DAVID LANZ

French Impressions

Art direction and cover design by Kristin Marie Lanz

Oridinal cover painting by Zoe Emmy
Editing by Kathy Parsons

Original recording of French Impressions piano improvisations available at **Davidlanz.com**

David Lanz is a Kawai Shigeru Piano Artist

ISBN: 978-1-5400-2757-3

Contact Us:
Hal Leonard
7777 West Bluemound Road
Milwaukee, WI 53213
Email: info@halleonard.com

In Europe contact:
Hal Leonard Europe Limited
42 Wigmore Street
Marylebone, London, W1U 2RN
Email: info@halleonardeurope.com

In Australia contact:
Hal Leonard Australia Pty. Ltd.
4 Lentara Court
Cheltenham, Victoria, 3192 Australia
Email: info@halleonard.com.au

T0055846

THE WANDERING PATH

By DAVID LANZ
and KRISTIN AMARIE LANZ

Moving freely and quickly

With pedal

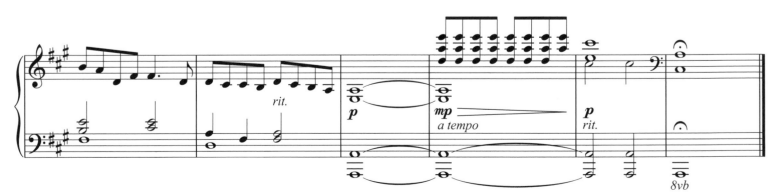

THE RIVER AT NIGHT

By DAVID LANZ
and KRISTIN AMARIE LANZ

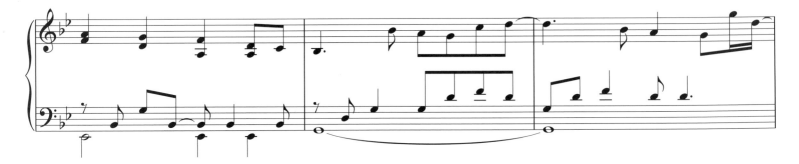

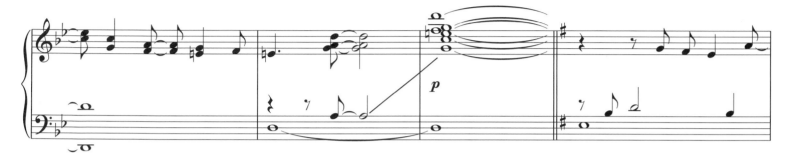

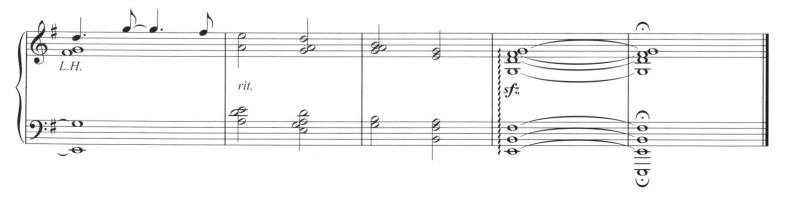

CONVERSATION AVEC LES ÉTOILES

By DAVID LANZ
and KRISTIN AMARIE LANZ

Moderately slow and expressive

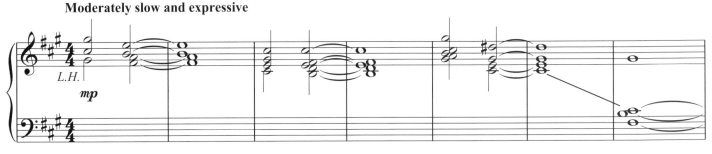

With generous pedal

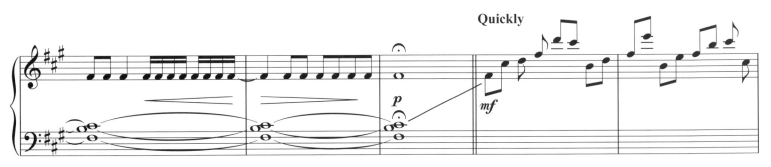

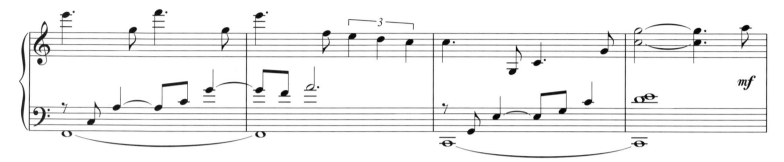

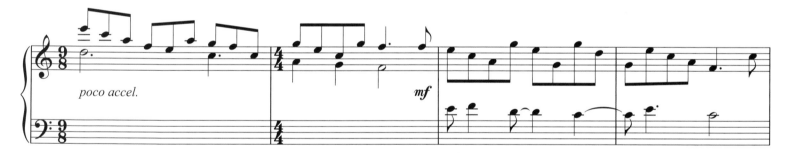

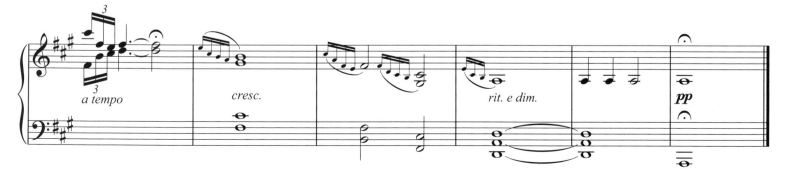

MIDNIGHT KISS

By DAVID LANZ
and KRISTIN AMARIE LANZ

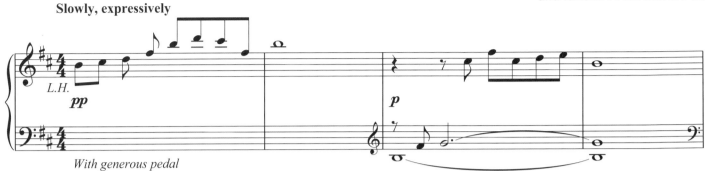

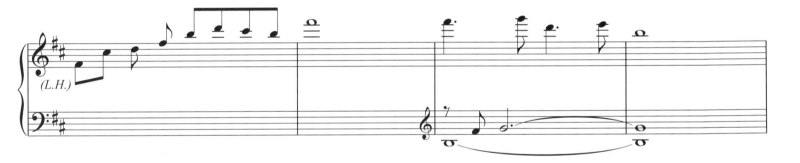

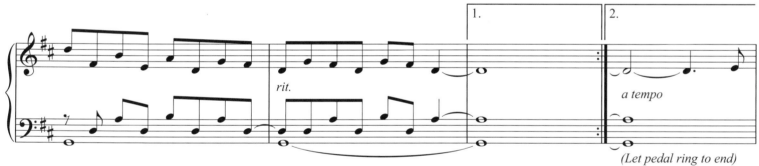

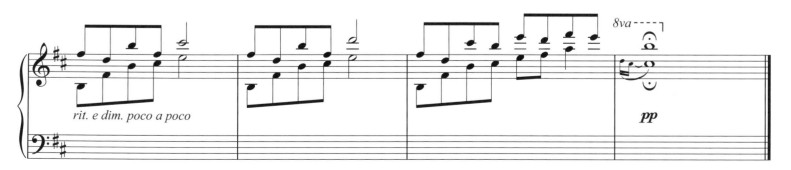

STILL LIFE #2

By DAVID LANZ
and KRISTIN AMARIE LANZ

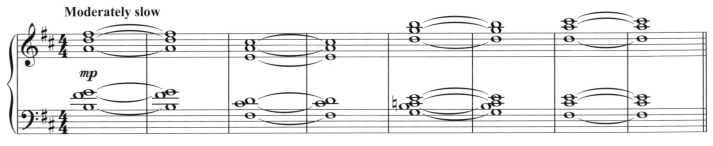

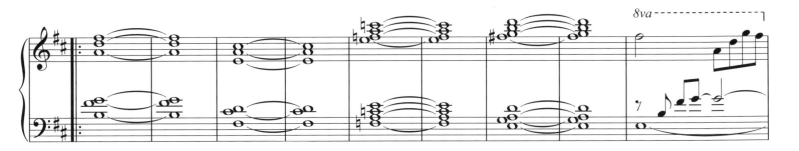

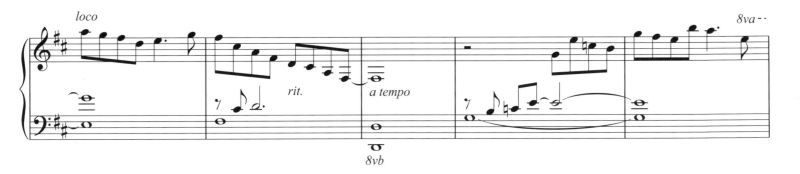

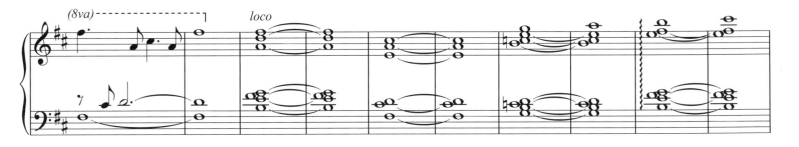

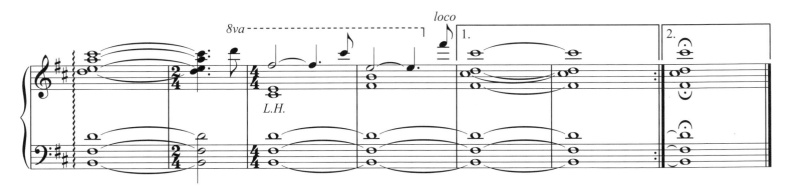

MARÉES DE MATIN

By DAVID LANZ
and KRISTIN AMARIE LANZ

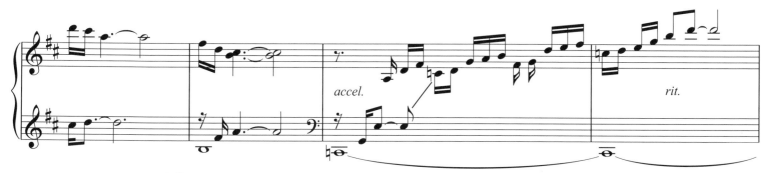

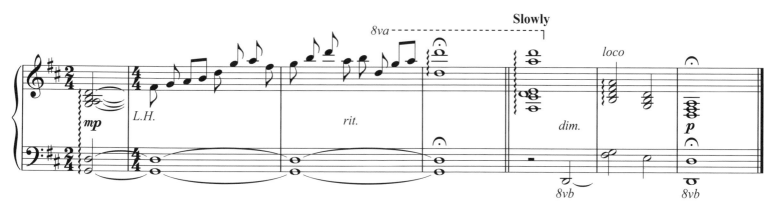

LOVE IS TRUTH

By DAVID LANZ
and KRISTIN AMARIE LANZ

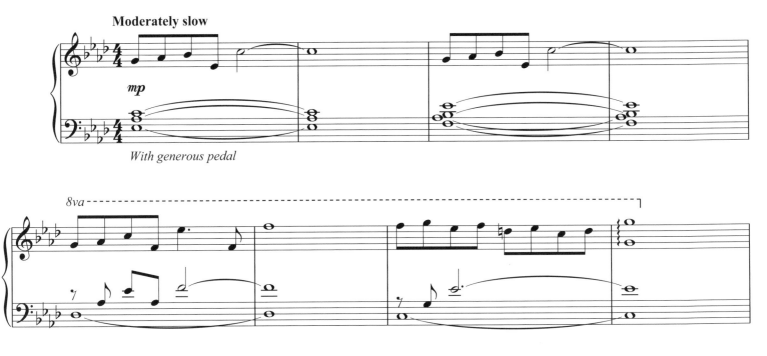

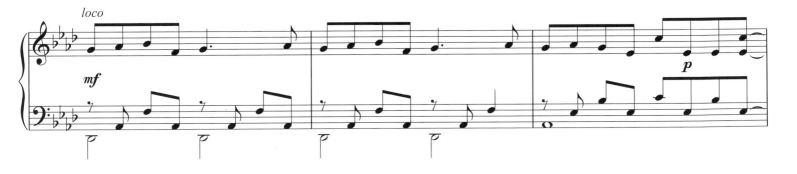

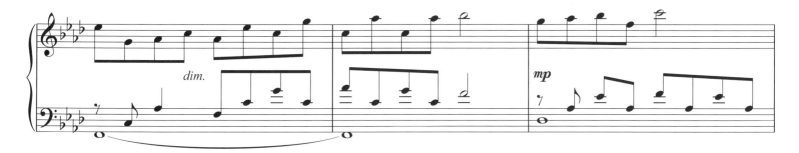

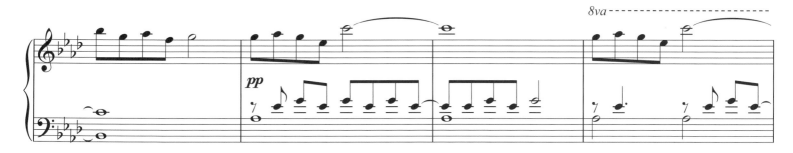

FRENCH BLUE

By DAVID LANZ
and KRISTIN AMARIE LANZ

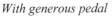

With generous pedal

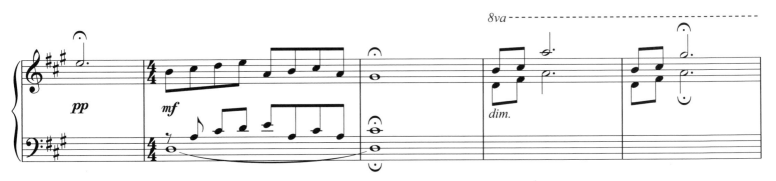

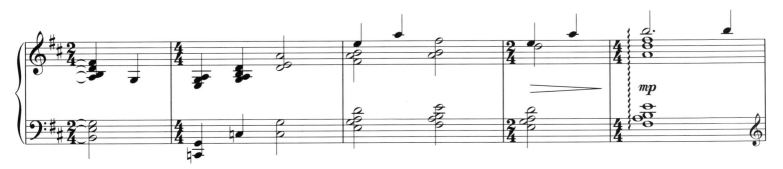

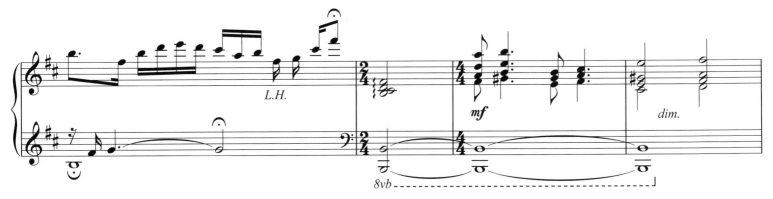

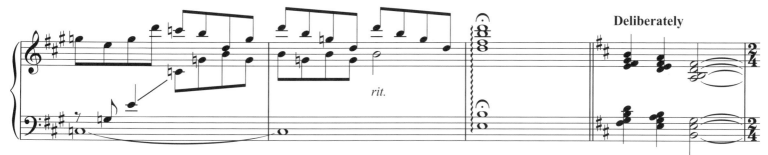

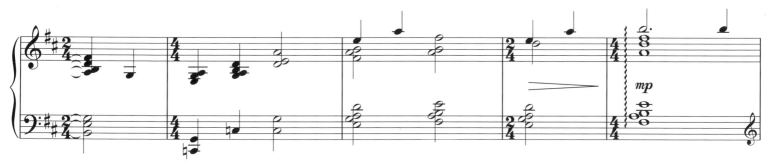

PASSAGES

By DAVID LANZ
and KRISTIN AMARIE LANZ

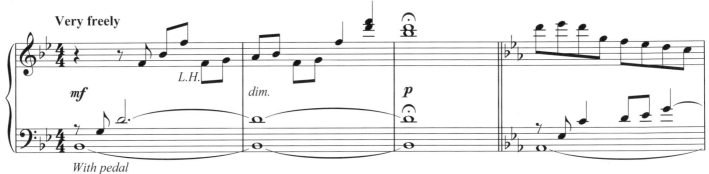

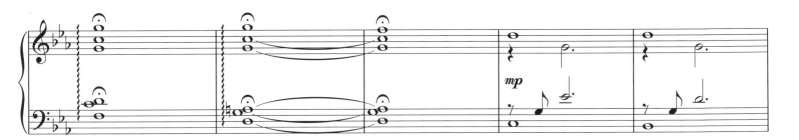

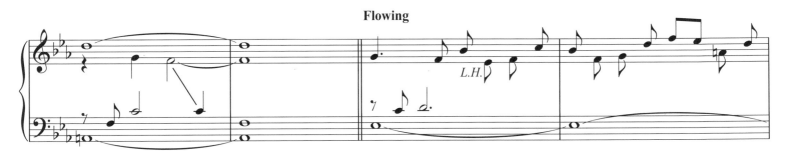

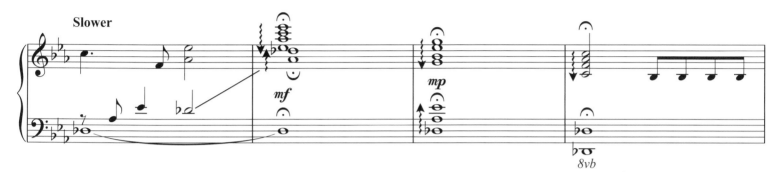

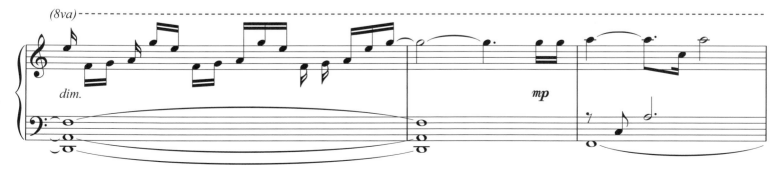

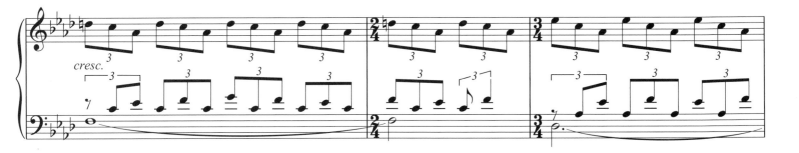

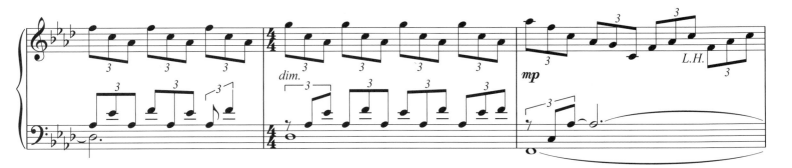

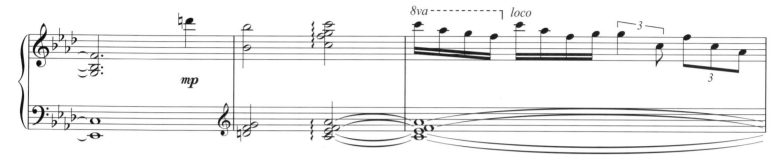

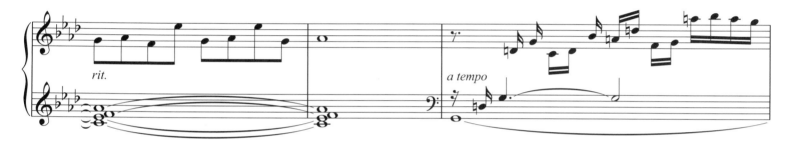

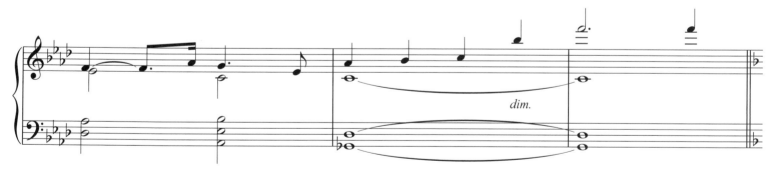

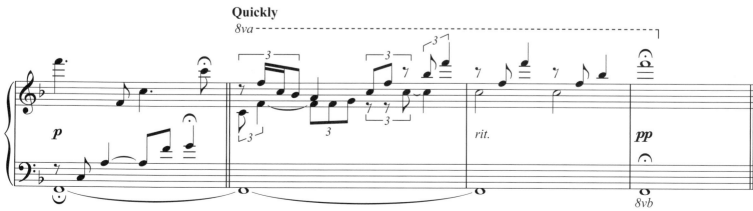

AS DREAMS DANCE

By DAVID LANZ
and KRISTIN AMARIE LANZ

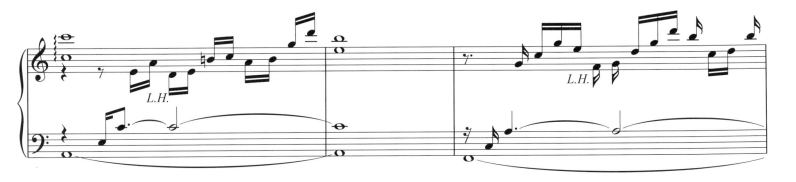

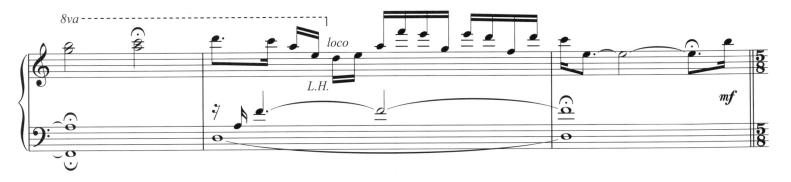

Slower, freely

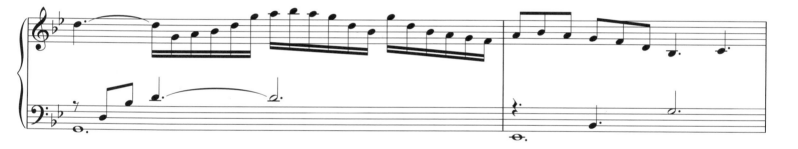

Slow, steady tempo

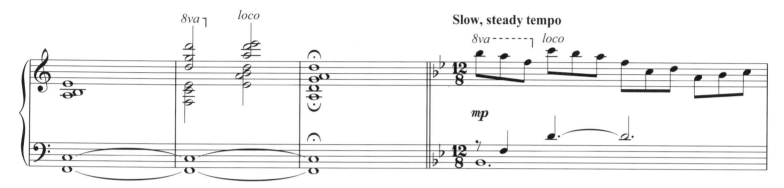

FRENCH IMPRESSIONS

By DAVID LANZ
and KRISTIN AMARIE LANZ

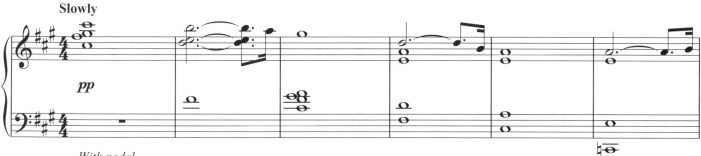

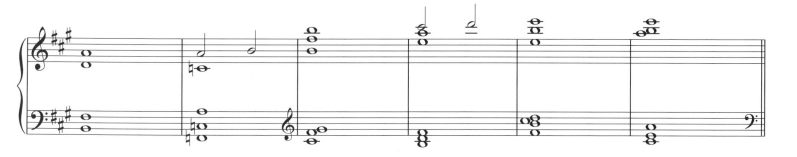

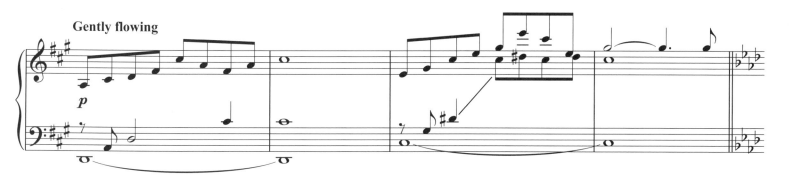

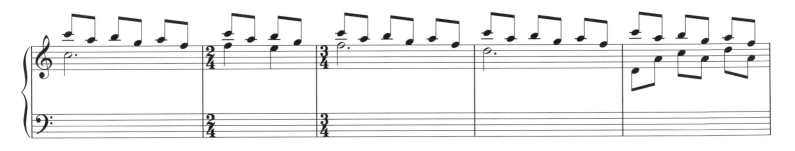

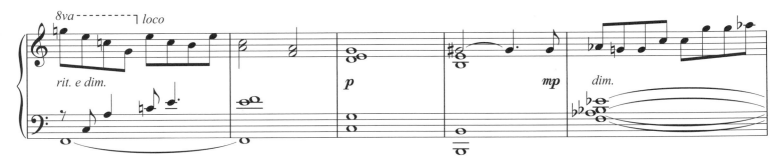

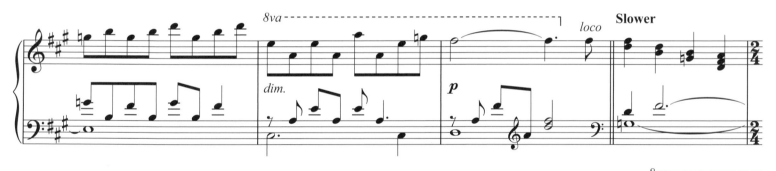

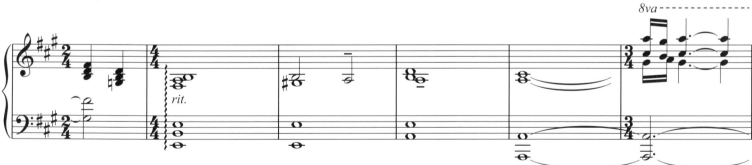

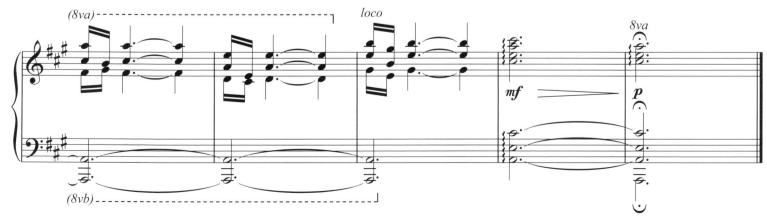

PRIÈRES DU SOIR

By DAVID LANZ
and KRISTIN AMARIE LANZ

Moderately slow and expressive

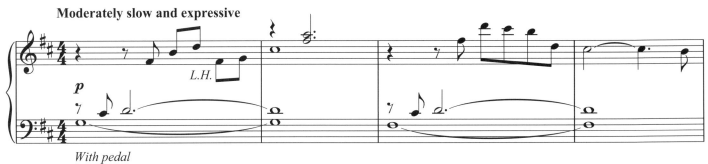

With pedal

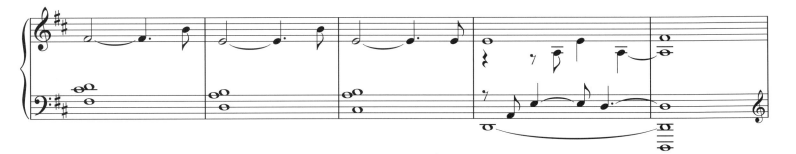

Flowing

Tempo I

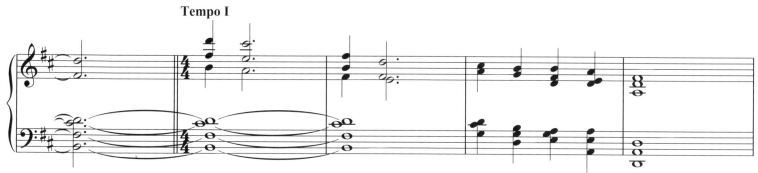

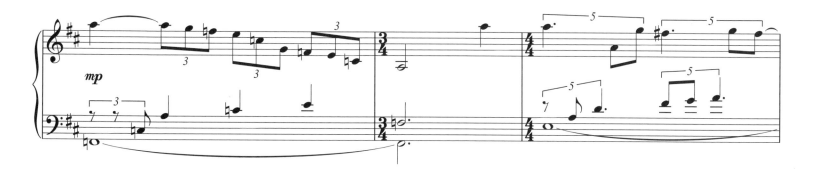

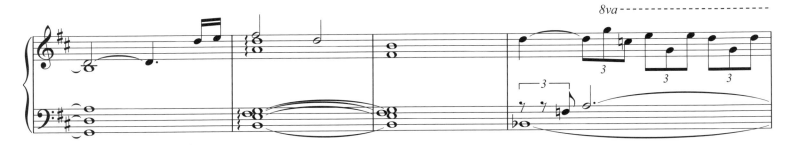

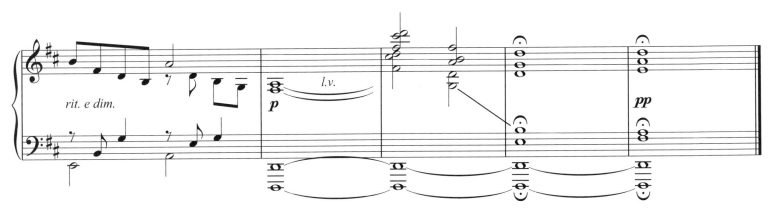